Amazon Echo

The Ultimate User Guide to Master Amazon Echo In No Time (Alexa Skills Kit, Amazon Echo 2016, user manual, web services, Free books, Free Movie, Alexa Kit)

ANDREW BUTLER

ISBN: 1533569703
ISBN-13: 978-1533569707

CONTENTS

I think next books will also be interesting for you:

Amazon Echo

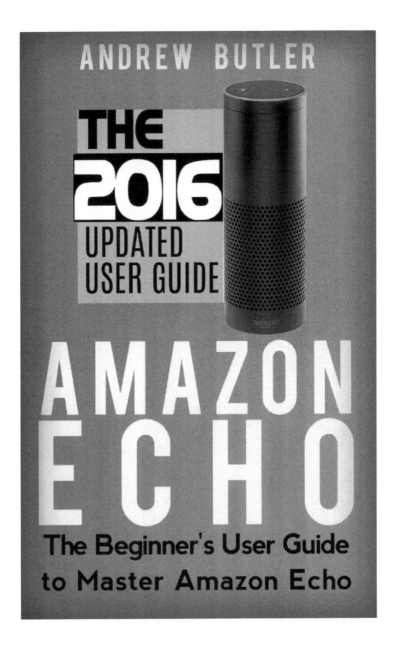

Amazon Echo

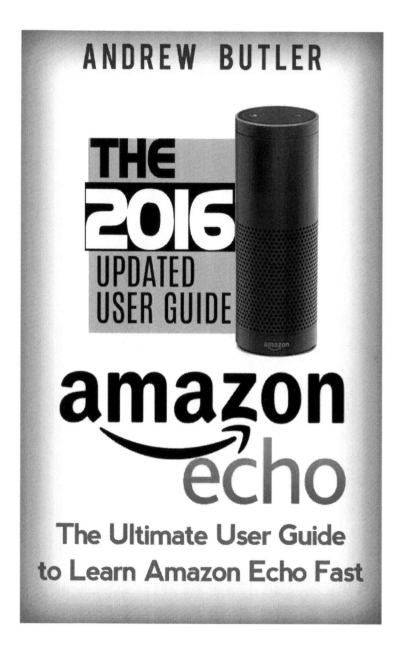

Windows 10

<u>Windows 10</u>

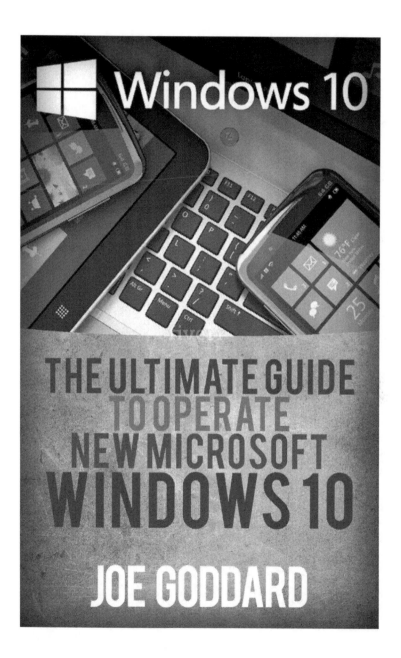

Amazon Prime and Kindle Lending Library

Introduction

Amazon Echo is undeniable a step into the future. Originally released in November 2015, Echo has already developed in leaps and bounds. With Amazon and individual developers continuously evolving the cloud-based voice recognition software, Alexa. There is no doubt about it, there's lot to envy about Echo.

The digital assistant that is Alexa will help you organize your life in a variety of aspects. Alexa can manage your alarms, calendars and to-do lists.

Not only that, but Alexa can help you with your shopping, although this feature is currently limited to Amazon.com, it is only a matter of time before Amazon extend this feature, if only to appease its users.

Whether you play tunes from your music library or stream them from your music streaming device, Alexa can add the soundtrack to your home whatever your mood.

There's plenty more to learn about Alexa, including how Echo can integrate with your smart home devices. In this simple guide we will teach you all about the basics and supply you with exactly what you need to say to get to grips with Alexa. Step into the world of Alexa and 'hands-free' your life in more ways than you can imagine.

Chapter 1 – Getting Started: The Basics

Set Up

Amazon Echo is built for a simple, sharp and seamless set up.

First things first, before you install your Echo at home, **download the Alexa App**. Free to download from appropriate app stores or from http://alexa.amazon.com for desktop users. The Alexa App will let you change a variety of settings with your Echo and is the secondary way to communicate with Alexa.

Once you've downloaded the Alexa App, install Echo into your home. Find a **suitable location** that meets the requirements - at least 8 inches (20cm) from any walls, windows or other electronic devices that could cause interference (e.g. your microwave). Once Echo is homed, plug the adapter in and then connect to the power outlet.

Echo's light ring will glow blue before turning orange at which point Alexa will greet you.

Next, **connect to Wi-Fi**. Echo can't connect to mobile hotspots or Ad-hoc (peer to peer) networks. Follow the next steps to connect your Echo with a Wi-Fi network.

1) Open the Alexa App > Open the left-hand-side navigation panel > Choose *Settings* from the options > Select your device > Choose *Set up a new device*.

2) On your Echo device press and hold the *Action* button for 5 seconds. This will change the Light Ring to orange whilst your device connects.

3) Return to the Alexa App - a list of Wi-Fi networks available for you to connect to will appear. If your Network does not appear choose *Rescan* or *Add a Network* from the bottom of the list.

Before you start using Alexa, **choose your wake word.** Your wake word is how Alexa knows you want/need something. The default settings mean Echo will respond to Alexa but if you want to you can change this to either Echo or Amazon. To do this follow these steps:

1) Open the Alexa App > Open the left-hand-side navigation panel > Select *Settings* > Choose your

device> Scroll through the options> Select *Wake Word* > From the drop down menu chose your desired wake word > Select Save >The light ring will briefly flash orange.

The Light Ring

To visually communicate with you, Echo has a light ring situated on its top. Beaming light in a variety of colors and arrangements, Echo can visually display Alexa's status. See the table below for some of Echo's light ring codes.

Color or Light Arrangement Visible	What this means
Solid blue with spinning cyan lights	Echo is starting up

All lights off	Echo is active and ready for requests
Orange light spinning clockwise	Echo is connecting to your Wi-Fi network
Continuous oscillating violet light	An error occurred during Wi-Fi setup.
Solid red light	The microphones are off. (Press the microphone button to turn on the microphones.)
White light	You are adjusting Echo's volume level.

Power LED

Also situated at the top of Echo is the Power Led. This visually shares Echo's Wi-Fi connection status with you. A solid white light means that your device has a Wi-Fi connection.

A solid orange light means there is no Wi-Fi connection. A blinking orange light means that your device is connected to Wi-Fi but cannot access Alexa.

Microphone off Button

Found at the top of Echo is the microphone off button. When pressed this allows you to turn off the Echo's seven microphones. On doing this the light ring will turn red.

Action Button

Similarly found on top of Echo is the action button which wakes Alexa. Use this to also turn off a timer, an alarm and put Echo into Wi-Fi setup mode if held for five seconds.

Volume Ring

By turning the volume ring clockwise Alexa's volume will increase, turn counter-clockwise for the volume to decrease. The light ring will display the volume level.

Bluetooth Settings

Echo comes built with Bluetooth compatibility which means you can connect to your mobile device by simply using the command *"Pair"*. Ensure that the Bluetooth on your mobile device is activated and in Echo's range before you request Alexa to pair. Alexa will notify you once you have successfully paired. To disconnect say *"Disconnect"*. It's that easy!

Using Multiple Devices

At this time there is no way to connect Alexa enabled devices so that they perform the same function. However using the Alexa App you can manage up to 12 different Alexa-enabled devices. So long as each one is registered to your Amazon account. Here are some helpful tips on how to use multiple Alexa-enabled devices.

For Echo and Echo Dot -choose different wake words for devices that are installed within speaking range of each other. If different devices have the same wake word make sure that they are at least 30 feet apart. Use the Alexa App or the Voice Remote for Amazon Echo to request/command one specific device.

For Fire TV Devices and Amazon Tap- give each device a distinct name.

Content sharing across Alexa devices is an areas which does require some improvement from Amazon. Currently you can view all the content which is shared between devices on the Alexa App in the settings menu. But, you are unable to customize which content is available to which device. Content that is shared across your Amazon account includes:

➢ Flash briefing

➢ Household profiles

- ➢ Music and media

- ➢ Shopping

- ➢ Smart Home Devices

- ➢ To Do Lists

Content that is not shared across your Amazon account includes:

- ➢ Alarms

- ➢ Bluetooth connections

- ➢ Sounds

- ➢ Wake Words

Software Updates

Alike all pieces of software, Alexa updates should be expected and continuously looked for. Before downloading the latest software you should check which version you have installed. To do this:

Open Alexa App > Open the left hand side navigation panel > Choose *Settings* > Select your device > Scroll down until *Device Software Version* is displayed.

To download the most recent software update ensure that your Echo is switched on and has an active Wi-Fi connection.

Then, avoid requesting/commanding anything from your device whilst the new software installs.

The light ring will turn blue once the update is ready to be installed. The time it takes to install the software update will vary and can depend on the speed of your Wi-Fi connection.

Chapter 2 – All About Alexa

Alexa is a cloud-based, voice recognition software. Activated using your desired wake word, you can ask Alexa a question such as *"What is the weather in London today?"* Or you can ask Alexa to do something like *"Add olives to my shopping list"* or *"play Coldplay's new album"*. You can even connect Alexa to your smart home devices and control your thermostat, lights, power outlets and more using just Alexa and your voice. For instance you could say *"Alexa, turn off the lights in the bedroom"* and they would turn off.

Just like a search engine you can review your voice interactions with Alexa. To do this: Open Alexa App > Choose Settings (from the left hand side navigation panel) > Select History.

By reviewing your interactions with Alexa you can help to improve how Alexa understands. You can also give feedback on inaccurate translations through the Alexa App.

In the same location of the Alexa App you can also delete voice interactions with Alexa from your History. To do this, tap an entry and the choose *Delete*.

The Alexa Skills Kit is free to download and will allow you to personalize and extend your Echo experience beyond all limits. If you want to access Alexa skills that have been developed and published you can view, enable and disable them all by visiting the Alexa App. It is also worth noting that in the *Skills* section of the Alexa App you can access a whole host of information about a skill, from invocation phrases, to developer details.

Here's a list of **questions** you can ask Alexa:

➤ *"Alexa, what is the weather here tomorrow?"*

➤ *"Alexa, when is Mother's Day this year?"*

➤ *"Alexa, what is fifteen times twelve?"*

➤ *"Alexa, what is capital of Zimbabwe?"*

➤ *"Alexa, how far is Jupiter?"*

➤ *"Alexa, who was the first President of America?"*

➤ *"Alexa, how old is Morgan Freeman?"*

➤ *"Alexa, who wrote Harry Potter?"*

➤ *"Alexa, who is the lead singer of Coldplay?"*

➤ *"Alexa, what is the IMDB rating for Game of Thrones?"*

➤ *"Alexa, how far is London from here?"*

> ➢ *"Alexa, Wikipedia: "Angelina Jolie"*

Get Weather Forecasts

Alexa uses AccuWeather for the latest weather information and can provide this to you dependent on your location.

To begin, you need to set up the location of your Alexa Device. Open the Alexa App > Open the left hand side navigation panel > Select *Settings* > Choose your device > Select *Edit* in *Device Location* > Enter the address > Select *Save.*

Once your location is set up you can ask Alexa:

> ➢ *"Alexa, what's the weather?"*

> ➢ *"Alexa,   what's   the   weather   for   this week/day/weekend?"*

> ➢ *"Alexa, will it rain tomorrow?"*

You can also ask Alexa about the weather in another location, to do this ask:

> ➢ *"Alexa, what's the weather in [city, county, state, country]?"*

Get News Updates

To hear the latest news simply ask Alexa:

> ➢ *"Alexa, what's in the news"*

Get Traffic Updates

Alexa can help you to plan your journey, giving you estimated journey lengths and finding you the quickest route depending on the current traffic status.

Firstly Open the Alexa App > Open the left hand side navigation panel > Select *Settings* > Choose *Traffic* > Select *Change address* in the *To* and *From* sections > Click *Save Changes.*

Once you have set your destination you can ask Alexa:

> ➢ *"Alexa, how is the traffic?"*

> ➢ *"Alexa, what's the traffic like right now?"*

> ➢ *"Alexa, what's my commute?"*

Your Calendar

Alexa can not only add events to your calendar but also and recall events that both you and others shared with your calendar. To do this you will first need to link you Google account to Alexa through the Alexa App.

> *"Alexa, what's on my calendar?"*

> *"Alexa, what's on my calendar Monday?"*

> *"Alexa, when is my next event?"*

> *"Alexa, add Go Swimming with Jane to my calendar for Monday, July 8th at 8pm.*

Search for Nearby Places

Alexa uses your device location and Yelp to find services that are located nearby you. Before you can use this feature you will need to make sure your device location is accurate. To do this:

Open the Alexa App > Open the left hand side navigation panel > Select *Settings* > Choose *Traffic* > Select *Change address* in the *To* and *From* sections > Click *Save Changes*.

Once your location is set you can ask Alexa to search for a variety of businesses, restaurants and shops. Ask Alexa for the address, phone number and hours of business for nearby places and more. For instance you could say:

> *"Alexa, what businesses are nearby?"*

> ➤ *"Alexa, find the address for the nearby [restaurant/business name]"*

> ➤ *"Alexa, find the opening hours for the nearby [restaurant/business name]"*

> ➤ *"Alexa, how far is [restaurant/business name]?"*

> ➤ *"Alexa, what is the phone number for [restaurant/business name]?"*

Setting Your Alarms and Timers

Alexa allows you to set timers and multiple one-off and repeating alarms. To set, confirm and cancel timers and alarms ask Alexa:

> ➤ *"Alexa, set alarm for 6 am?"*

> ➤ *"Alexa, when is my alarm set for?"*

> ➤ *"Alexa, what time is it?"*

> ➤ *"Alexa, set the timer for 15 minutes"*

> ➤ *"Alexa, how much time is left on my timer?"*

> ➤ *"Alexa, cancel my alarm for tomorrow"*

You can also use Alexa to stop or snooze your alarm when it goes off. To do this say:

> ➤ *"Alexa, stop"*

> ➤ *"Alexa, snooze"*

You can determine the volume and tone of your timer and alarms through the Alexa App. Firstly > Open the Alexa App > Open the left hand navigation panel > Select *Settings* > Chose your device > Select *Sounds* > Chose *Alarm and Timer Volume.*

Managing Lists

Alexa can help you keep organized. With the ability to list up to 100 items on each list, you can view your lists on your desktop, (the Amazon website), the Alexa App and even print them out.

To **open a list** > Open the mobile Alexa App > Open the left hand side navigation panel > Select *Shopping and To-Do Lists* > Select your desired list and view.

You can request Alexa to **review and add items** to your existing lists by saying:

> ➢ *"Alexa, what's on my To-Do List?"*

> ➢ *"Alexa, what's on my Shopping List?"*

> ➢ *"Alexa, add [item] to my Shopping list."*

> ➢ *"Alexa, put [task] onto my To-do List."*

In the Alexa App you can also **mark items as complete** to do this > Open the Alexa App > Open the left hand side navigation menu > Select *Shopping and To-Do Lists* > Choose the list you want > Select a checkbox next to an item.

To **view only your completed items** > Open the Alexa App > Open the left hand side navigation menu > Select *Shopping and To-Do Lists* > Choose the list you want > Select *View Completed*.

To **print a list** > Open the Alexa App on your desktop > Open the left hand side navigation menu > Select *Shopping and To-Do Lists* > Choose the list you want to print > Select *Print* > Follow the instructions provided by your web browser.

Smart Home Devices

Alexa can integrate with a number of smart home devices. Devices that Alexa can operate include; lights, fans, thermostats, doors, locks, power outlets and appliances. To use a smart home device with Alexa ensure that you follow the instructions and recommendations that are given by the device manufacture.

Before connecting your smart home device with Alexa, download the companion app > Set up the smart home device so that is uses the same Wi-Fi network as Alexa > Ensure that your device is running the latest software.

To connect your smart home device with Alexa you will need to:

Open the Alexa app > Open the left hand navigation panel > Choose *Skills* > Select *Refine* > Choose *Smart Home Skills* > Search for the skill your smart home device requires > Select *Enable* > Sign in using your third party log in details (details for the smart device) if required > Save > Say "Alexa, discover my devices" or select *Discover devices* from the Alexa App.

Once you have linked your smart home device with Alexa you can control and operate it using your voice by saying:

> *"Alexa, turn on [smart home device name]"*

> *"Alexa, turn off [smart home device]"*

> *"Alexa, set brightness to [?]%"* - This can only be used with compatible lights that allow you to change the brightness.

> *"Alexa, set [thermostat name] temperature to [?] degrees"*

> *"Alexa, raise/lower the [thermostat name/room name] temperature"*

> *"Alexa, turn the lights on in [room name]"*

> *"Alexa, turn the fan on in [room name]"*

> *"Alexa, set the fan to [?]%"*

By using the Alexa Skills Kit you can create skills that will integrate your smart home device with Alexa - should skills not be available for your requirements. To find smart home skills that are available to you and your device:

Open the Alexa App > Open the left hand side navigation panel > Select *Skills* > Choose *Refine* > Select *Smart Home Skills*.

Chapter 3 – Music Matters

With Echo, music matters. Whenever, wherever* if you want to listen to Music on your Alexa device all you need to do is ask. You don't even need to have the song, album, or artist in your music library because Alexa can search the Prime Music catalog to find you exactly what your ears want to hear.

*So long as you are within Alexa's hearing capabilities.

The commands you need to know get Alexa playing are:

➢ Adjust the volume - "*Volume up/ Volume Down*"

➢ To hear details about the track currently playing - "*Who is this?*" or "*What song is this*" or "*Which artist sings this?*"

➢ Play a song - "*Play the song [song name]*" or "*Play some music*"

➢ Play an album - "*Play the album [album name]*"

➢ Play music by an artist - "*Play songs by [artist name]*"

➢ Play songs from a genre - "*Play some [genre name] music*"

➢ Play a playlist- "*Listen to my [playlist name] playlist*"

➢ Play songs that have been paused or stopped - "*Play*" or "*Resume*"

➢ Stop the track that is playing - "*Stop*" or "*Pause*"

➢ Go to the next or previous track - "*Next*" or "*Previous*"

➤ Repeat songs - *"Repeat"*

➤ Look the music queue - *"Loop"*

➤ Shuffle songs or tracks of an album or playlist - *"Shuffle"* and *"Stop Shuffle"*

Streaming Music Services

With Echo you can also listen to streaming music services. These include Spotify Premium, iHeartRadio and Pandora. Before you can play music from your streaming service and through Alexa you will need to link these services together. To do this:

Open Alexa App > Open the left hand side navigation panel > Choose *Music and Books* > Choose your streaming service from the options > Select *Link account to Alexa* > Sign into your account (using the login details you signed up to your music streaming service with) > Once you have logged in Alexa and your music streaming service should be connected.

If your account fails to connect try resetting your login details and then linking your account to Alexa again.

To **unlink your account** > Open the Alexa App > Open the left hand side navigation panel > Choose *Music and Books* >

Choose your streaming service from the options > Select Unlink

Once you have successfully linked your account with Alexa you can request Alexa to stream music at your leisure. To this you will need the following commands:

- Play Prime Music - *"Play Prime Music"*

- Play Spotify Premium - *"Play Spotify Premium"*

- Play a radio station - *"Play [station frequency]"* or *"Play [station name]"*

- Play a custom station - *"Play my [artist/genre] station on [Pandora/iHeartRadio/Prime Music]"*

- Play a podcast or program - *"Play the podcast [podcast name]/"* or *"Play the program [program name]"*

- Skip to the next song - *"Skip"*

- Like / Dislike a song - *"I like this song /I don't like this song"or "Thumbs up/ Thumbs down"*

➤ Take a frequently played song off the playlist/out of rotation (Pandora and Prime Stations only) - *"I'm tired of this song"*

Buying Music

Not only can you play music from your music library and stream music from your streaming service but now with Alexa you can also purchase music. If you have a valid U.S billing address and U.S bank issued or U.S Amazon.com Gift Card you can access this service. Unfortunately, at this time this service is not available to people that do not meet this requirements.

Note: Before you can begin shopping you will first need to update your **voice purchasing settings**. See Chapter 4 for how to do this.

Brought to you through Amazon's Digital Music Store you can purchase music and pay using Echo's 1-click payment method. Purchases that you make from the Digital Music Store are saved in your music library and don't count toward storage limits. Plus, purchases can be played back as much or as little as like and you can also access and download them onto any device that supports Amazon Music.

To edit the settings that enable, disable and identify whether you require a confirmation code for purchasing > Open the Alexa App > Open the left hand side navigation panel > Choose *Settings* > Select *Voice* > Choose *Purchasing*.

Alexa will always notify you of any additional costs when purchasing music.

Once you have set Echo up to purchase music for you through the Alexa App you will need the following commands:

> To shop for a song or album - *"Shop for the song [song name]"*

> To shop for songs by a particular artist - *"Shop for songs by [artists name]"*

> To purchase the song currently playing - *"Buy this [song/album]"*

> To add the song currently playing to your playlist - *"Add this [song/album] to my library"*

Chapter 4 – Spotlight on Shopping

Just as you can ask Alexa to play music you can ask Alexa to help you with your shopping. For all aspects of shopping through Alexa you will need an Amazon account.

Currently you can only purchase items through Amazon.com. This can be items you have previously purchased, items that are top Prime products and digital music and albums.

Before you can begin shopping you will first need to update your **voice purchasing settings**. Note, that by default voice purchasing is set to 'on'. To do this:

Open the Alexa App > Open the left hand side navigation panel > Choose *Settings* > Select *Voice Purchasing*.

> ➢ Toggle the *Purchase by voice* option to turn voice purchasing on or off.

➢ You can enable *Require confirmation code,* this means that you will need to supply a 4-digit confirmation code before each and every order > Enter a 4-digit code > Select *Save Changes.* Although you will have to supply your 4-digit code by voice before purchasing it will not appear in your voice history.

➢ From the *Voice Purchasing* settings you can also manage 1-click settings, to do this select *Go To Amazon.com* and set your payment method and billing address.

To purchase **Physical Products** you will need to have previously ordered them from Amazon.com. You will also need an annual membership or 30-day free trial of Amazon Prime.

Once Alexa has found the item you will then need to confirm or cancel the order. If Alexa finds two items which fulfill the request, Alexa will offer the second item after you have declined the first.

If Alexa can't find an item in your history Alexa might offer you an item from Amazon's Choice. Amazon's Choice is a list of items that have high ratings and are well priced with Prime shipping.

If Alexa can't find your item and doesn't offer you an Amazon's Choice, Alexa will add the item you requested to your Amazon.com shopping list account.

If you have multiple orders waiting to be delivered, Alexa will give you the information of the order that is closest to being delivered.

Some of the commands you need to purchase and re-order items through Amazon are:

> To reorder an item - *"Reorder [item name]"* or *"Yes/No"* when Alexa asks you to confirm the product found.

- To add an item to your shopping cart - *"Add [item name] to my cart"*

- To track the status of an order that has recently been shipped - *"Track my order"* or *"Where is my stuff"*

- To cancel an order - *"Cancel my order"* - Note you can only do this immediately after you have confirmed an order.

Remember that you can always visit Amazon.com on your mobile device or desktop to confirm, edit and cancel any orders you make through Alexa should you need to.

Returns

The full return policy for products purchased through Alexa can be found at: https://www.amazon.com/gp/help/customer/display.html?nodeId=15015721

Non-digital products that are purchased using Alexa are automatically eligible for free returns. If you accidently purchase a song or album from the Amazon Digital Music Store you can request a return and refund but, your request must be received by Amazon Customer Service within seven days.

Chapter 5 – Extras

1. Access Echo Online

Yes, the Alexa App is quick, simple and very easy to access but if for whatever reason you can't access the Alexa App just visit http://echo.amazon.com

2. Ask Alexa Funny Questions

Just alike other voice recognition software you can ask Alexa a variety of questions to which Alexa will respond with comical and witty answers. Try out these:

➤ *"Alexa, is Santa real?"*

➤ *"Alexa, what is love?"*

➤ *"Alexa, I want the truth?"*

➤ *"Alexa, is this the real life?"*

➢ *"Alexa, I have a cold?"*

➢ *"Alexa, you complete me"*

➢ *"Alexa, to be or not to be?"*

3. The Alexa App

The Alexa App is the go-to tool to help you set up Echo and Alexa. Available on your mobile device and through your desktop and web browser Alexa has everything you need to customize and control Alexa hands on.

Here is a short list of what each feature in the Alexa App navigation panel does.

Note: To find the navigation panel > Open the Alexa App > On the left hand side if a Menu icon > Select this.

➢ Help and Feedback - Here you will find in depth help information for your Echo device. You can also submit feedback about your experience with Alexa, good or bad.

➢ Home - Show you your voice history with Alexa

➢ Music and Books - This allows you to search for songs, radio stations, shows, Kindle Books and audiobooks that you can listen to through Echo.

➢ Now Playing - Shows you the track you are currently playing, the tracks that are upcoming and the ones previously played.

➤ Not [Name]? Sign Out - Click here to sign out of the Alexa App

➤ Settings - In this sub section you will find everything you need to set up your Echo device, you will find various Alexa device settings and you can train Alexa to understand your speech patterns and annunciations.

➤ Shopping & To Do Lists - Here you can view, manage and edit your shopping and to-do lists.

➤ Skills - You can search for, enable and disable skills that you want Alexa to possess. You can also view all the information about skills from invocation phrases to developer details.

➤ Smart Home - Here you can manage all the settings you need to for smart home devices that you want to/have linked to Alexa.

➤ Times and Alarms - You can view, edit and delete timers and alarms set by Alexa,

➤ Things to Try - Here you will find a list of example phrases that you can ask Alexa.

Conclusion

This guide covers the simplest of set up and gets you going with the skeleton of how Echo works. Starting with plugging in, Wi-Fi connection, Bluetooth pairing and the physical hardware.

You should now know what Alexa is and how to use it. We have given you an insight into productivity by creating alarms, times and managing To-Do and Shopping Lists, a nod to a more organized and efficient life. Which, surely can't be a bad thing.

Alexa can give you the soundtrack to your life, whatever the occasion and mood and by following our easy step by step instructions you should be well on your way to making every moment musical. Not only that, but we've explained how you and Echo can shop together. A skill that is bound to expand.

Paired with Alexa's universal knowledge and growing skills; Echo can help you with every question, request and command and boasting seven built in microphones and 360° immersive sound, the Echo device is all in all - a rival that no competitor wants to fight.

Over time, Alexa will develop. Smart homes may well become society's norm and the unfathomable potential of cloud-based voice recognition software will have been unleashed. What more is there to say? You've got your foot, your head, and certainly your voice in the right direction by starting now.

Thank you for reading. I hope you enjoy it. I ask you to leave your honest feedback.

Made in the USA
Middletown, DE
24 October 2016